D1271995

SYMBOLISM

ALFRED NORTH WHITEHEAD

SYMBOLISM

Its Meaning and Effect

Barbour–Page Lectures
University of Virginia
1927

New York
FORDHAM UNIVERSITY PRESS
1985

LC 58–10916
ISBN 0–8232–1137–1 (*clothbound*)
ISBN 0–8232–1138–x (*paperback*)
First edition 1927
Reissued 1958
Reset line-for-line and republished 1985

Printed in the United States of America

DEDICATION

These chapters were written before I had seen the Washington monument which faces the Capitol in the City of Washington, and before I had enjoyed the experience of crossing the borders of the State of Virginia—a great experience for an Englishman.

Virginia, that symbol for romance throughout the world of English speech: Virginia, which was captured for that world in the romantic period of English history by Sir Walter Raleigh, its most romantic figure: Virginia, which has been true to its origin and has steeped its history in romance.

Romance does not yield unbroken happiness: Sir Walter Raleigh suffered for his romance. Romance does not creep along the ground; like the memorial to Washington, it reaches upward—a silver thread uniting earth to the blue of heaven above.

April 8, 1927

PREFACE

In accordance with the terms of the Barbour–Page Foundation, these lectures are published by the University of Virginia. The author owes his thanks to the authorities of the university for their courtesy in conforming to his wishes in respect to some important details of publication. With the exception of a few trifling changes the lectures are printed as delivered.

These lectures will be best understood by reference to some portions of Locke's *Essay Concerning Human Understanding*. The author's acknowledgments are due to *Locke's Theory of Knowledge and Its Historical Relations* by Professor James Gibson, to *Prolegomena to an Idealist Theory of Knowledge* by Professor Norman Kemp Smith, and to *Scepticism and Animal Faith* by George Santayana.

A. N. W.

Harvard University, June 1927

CONTENTS

CHAPTER I

CHAPTER III

SYMBOLISM,
ITS MEANING AND EFFECT

CHAPTER I

1. *Kinds of Symbolism*

The slightest survey of different epochs of civilization discloses great differences in their attitude towards symbolism. For example, during the medieval period in Europe symbolism seemed to dominate men's imaginations. Architecture was symbolical, ceremonial was symbolical, heraldry was symbolical. With the Reformation a reaction set in. Men tried to dispense with symbols as 'fond things, vainly invented,' and concentrated on their direct apprehension of the ultimate facts.

But such symbolism is on the fringe of life. It has an unessential element in its constitution. The very fact that it can be acquired in one epoch and discarded in another epoch testifies to its superficial nature.

There are deeper types of symbolism, in a sense artificial, and yet such that we could not get on without them. Language, written or spoken, is such a symbolism. The mere sound of a word, or its shape on paper, is indifferent. The word is a symbol, and its meaning is constituted by the ideas, images, and emotions, which it raises in the mind of the hearer.

There is also another sort of language, purely a written language, which is constituted by the mathematical symbols of the science of algebra. In some ways, these symbols are different to those of ordinary language, because the manipulation of the algebraical symbols does your reasoning for you, provided that you keep to the algebraic rules. This is not the case with ordinary language. You can never forget the meaning of language, and trust to mere syntax to help you out. In any case, language and algebra seem to exemplify more fundamental types of symbolism than do the Cathedrals of Medieval Europe.

2. *Symbolism and Perception*

There is still another symbolism more fundamental than any of the foregoing types. We look up and see a coloured shape in front of us, and we say,—there is a chair. But what we have seen is the mere coloured shape. Perhaps an artist might not have jumped to the notion of a chair. He might have stopped at the mere contemplation of a beautiful colour and a beautiful shape. But those of us who are not artists are very prone, especially if we are tired, to pass straight from the perception of the coloured shape to the enjoyment of the chair, in some way of use, or of emotion, or of thought. We can easily explain this passage by reference to a train of difficult logical inference, whereby, having regard to our previous experiences of various shapes and various colours, we draw the probable conclusion that we are in the presence of a chair. I am very sceptical as to the high-grade character of the mentality required to get from the coloured shape to the chair. One reason for this scepticism is that my friend the artist, who kept himself to the contemplation of colour, shape and position, was a very highly trained man, and had acquired this facility of ignoring the chair at the cost of great labour. We do not require elaborate training merely in order to refrain from embarking upon intricate trains of inference. Such abstinence is only too easy. Another reason for scepticism is that if we had been accompanied by a puppy dog, in addition to the artist, the dog would have acted immediately on the hypothesis of a chair and would have jumped onto it by way of using it as such.   Again, if the dog had refrained from such action, it would have been because it was a well-trained dog.   Therefore the transition from a coloured shape to the notion of an object which can be used for all sorts of purposes which have nothing to do with colour, seems to be a very natural one; and we—men and puppy dogs—require careful training if we are to refrain from acting upon it.

Thus coloured shapes seem to be symbols for some other elements in our experience, and when we see the coloured shapes we adjust our actions towards those other elements.   This symbolism from our senses to the bodies symbolized is often mistaken.   A cunning adjustment of lights and mirrors may completely deceive us; and even when we are not deceived, we only save ourselves by an effort.   Symbolism from sense-presentation to physical bodies is the most natural and widespread of all symbolic modes.   It is not a mere tropism, or automatic turning towards, because both men and puppies often disregard chairs when they see them. Also a tulip which turns to the light has probably the very minimum of sense-presentation. I shall argue on the assumption that sense-perception is mainly a characteristic of more advanced organisms; whereas all organisms have experience of causal efficacy whereby their functioning is conditioned by their environment.

3. On Methodology

In fact symbolism is very largely concerned with the use of pure sense-perceptions in the character of symbols for more primitive elements in our experience. Accordingly since sense-perceptions, of any importance, are characteristic of high-grade organisms, I shall chiefly confine this study of symbolism to the influence of symbolism on human life. It is a general principle that low-grade characteristics are better studied first in connection with correspondingly low-grade organisms, in which those characteristics are not obscured by more developed types of functioning. Conversely, high-grade characters should be studied first in connection with those organisms in which they first come to full perfection.

Of course, as a second approximation to elicit the full sweep of particular characters, we want to know the embryonic stage of the high-grade character, and the ways in which low-grade characters can be made subservient to higher types of functioning.

The nineteenth century exaggerated the power of the historical method, and assumed as a matter of course that every character should be studied only in its embryonic stage. Thus, for example, 'Love' has been studied among the savages and latterly among the morons.

4. *Fallibility of Symbolism*

There is one great difference between symbolism and direct knowledge. Direct experience is infallible. What you have experienced, you have experienced. But symbolism is very fallible, in the sense that it may induce actions, feelings, emotions, and beliefs about things which are mere notions without that exemplification in the world which the symbolism leads us to presuppose. I shall develop the thesis that symbolism is an essential factor in the way we function as the result of our direct knowledge. Successful high-grade organisms are only possible, on the condition that their symbolic functionings are usually justified so far as important issues are concerned. But the errors of mankind equally spring from symbolism. It is the task of reason to understand and purge the symbols on which humanity depends.

An adequate account of human mentality requires an explanation of (i) how we can know truly, (ii) how we can err, and (iii) how we can critically distinguish truth from error. Such an explanation requires that we distinguish that type of mental functioning which by its nature yields immediate acquaintance with fact, from that type of functioning which is only trustworthy by reason of its satisfaction of certain criteria provided by the first type of functioning.

I shall maintain that the first type of functioning is properly to be called 'Direct Recognition,' and the second type 'Symbolic Reference.' I shall also endeavour to illustrate the doctrine that all human symbolism, however superficial it may seem, is ultimately to be reduced to trains of this fundamental symbolic reference, trains which finally connect percepts in alternative modes of direct recognition.

5. Definition of Symbolism

After this prefatory explanation, we must start from a formal definition of symbolism: The human mind is functioning symbolically when some components of its experience elicit consciousness, beliefs, emotions, and usages, respecting other components of its experience. The former set of components are the 'symbols,' and the latter set constitute the 'meaning' of the symbols. The organic functioning whereby there is transition from the symbol to the meaning will be called 'symbolic reference.'

This symbolic reference is the active synthetic element contributed by the nature of the percipient. It requires a ground founded on some community between the natures of symbol and meaning. But such a common element in the two natures does not of itself necessitate symbolic reference, nor does it decide which shall be symbol and which shall be meaning, nor does it secure that the symbolic reference shall be immune from producing errors and disasters for the percipient. We must conceive perception in the light of a primary phase in the self-production of an occasion of actual existence.

In defence of this notion of self-production arising out of some primary given phase, I would remind you that, apart from it, there can be no moral responsibility. The potter, and not the pot, is responsible for the shape of the pot. An actual occasion arises as the bringing together into one real context diverse perceptions, diverse feelings, diverse purposes, and other diverse activities arising out of those primary perceptions. Here activity is another name for self-production.

6. *Experience as Activity*

In this way we assign to the percipient an activity in the production of its own experience, although that moment of experience, in its character of being that one occasion, is nothing else than the percipient itself. Thus, for the percipient at least, the perception is an internal relationship between itself and the things perceived.

In analysis the total activity involved in perception of the symbolic reference must be referred to the percipient. Such symbolic reference requires something in common between symbol and meaning which can be expressed without reference to the perfected percipient; but it also requires some activity of the percipient which can be considered without recourse either to the particular symbol or its particular meaning. Considered by themselves the symbol and its meaning do not require *either* that there shall be a symbolic reference between the two, *or* that the symbolic reference between the members of the couple should be one way on rather than the other way on. The nature of their relationship does not in itself determine which is symbol and which is meaning. There are no components of experience which are only symbols or only meanings. The more usual symbolic reference is from the less primitive component as symbol to the more primitive as meaning.

This statement is the foundation of a thoroughgoing realism. It does away with any mysterious element in our experience which is merely meant, and thereby behind the veil of direct perception. It proclaims the principle that symbolic reference holds between two components in a complex experience, each intrinsically capable of direct recognition. Any lack of such conscious analytical recognition is the fault of the defect in mentality on the part of a comparatively low-grade percipient.

7. *Language*

To exemplify the inversion of symbol and meaning, consider language and the things meant by language. A word is a symbol. But a word can be either written or spoken. Now on occasions a written word may suggest the corresponding spoken word, and that sound may suggest a meaning.

In such an instance, the written word is a symbol and its meaning is the spoken word, and the spoken word is a symbol and its meaning is the dictionary meaning of the word, spoken or written.

But often the written word effects its purpose without the intervention of the spoken word. Accordingly, then, the written word directly symbolizes the dictionary meaning. But so fluctuating and complex is human experience that in general neither of these cases is exemplified in the clear-cut way which is set out here. Often the written word suggests both the spoken word and also the meaning, and the symbolic reference is made clearer and more definite by the additional reference of the spoken word to the same meaning. Analogously we can start from the spoken word which may elicit a visual perception of the written word.

Further, why do we say that the word 'tree'—spoken or written—is a symbol to us for trees? Both the word itself and trees themselves enter into our experience on equal terms; and it would

be just as sensible, viewing the question abstract-
edly, for trees to symbolize the word 'tree' as for
the word to symbolize the trees.

This is certainly true, and human nature sometimes works that way. For example, if you are a
poet and wish to write a lyric on trees, you will
walk into the forest in order that the trees may
suggest the appropriate words. Thus for the poet
in his ecstasy—or perhaps, agony—of composition
the trees are the symbols and the words are the
meaning. He concentrates on the trees in order to
get at the words.

But most of us are not poets, though we read
their lyrics with proper respect. For us, the words
are the symbols which enable us to capture the
rapture of the poet in the forest. The poet is a
person for whom visual sights and sounds and
emotional experiences refer symbolically to words.
The poet's readers are people for whom his words
refer symbolically to the visual sights and sounds
and emotions he wants to evoke. Thus in the use
of language there is a double symbolic reference:
—from things to words on the part of the speaker,
and from words back to things on the part of the
listener.

When in an act of human experience there is a

symbolic reference, there are in the first place two sets of components with some objective relationship between them, and this relationship will vary greatly in different instances. In the second place the total constitution of the percipient has to effect the symbolic reference from one set of components, the symbols, to the other set of components, the meaning. In the third place, the question, as to which set of components forms the symbols and which set the meaning, also depends on the peculiar constitution of that act of experience.

8. *Presentational Immediacy*

The most fundamental exemplification of symbolism has already been alluded to in the discussion of the poet and the circumstances which elicit his poetry. We have here a particular instance of the reference of words to things. But this general relation of words to things is only a particular instance of a yet more general fact. Our perception of the external world is divided into two types of content: one type is the familiar immediate presentation of the contemporary world, by means of our projection of our immediate sensations, determining for us characteristics of contemporary physical entities. This type is the experience of the immediate world around us, a world decorated by sense-data dependent on the immediate states of relevant parts of our own bodies. Physiology establishes this latter fact conclusively; but the physiological details are irrelevant to the present philosophical discussion, and only confuse the issue. 'Sense-datum' is a modern term: Hume uses the word 'impression.'

For human beings, this type of experience is vivid, and is especially distinct in its exhibition of the spatial regions and relationships within the contemporary world.

The familiar language which I have used in speaking of the 'projection of our sensations' is very misleading. There are no bare sensations which are first experienced and then 'projected' into our feet as their feelings, or onto the opposite wall as its colour. The projection is an integral part of the situation, quite as original as the sense-data. It would be just as accurate, and equally misleading, to speak of a projection on the wall which is then characterized as such-and-such a colour. The use of the term 'wall' is equally misleading by its suggestion of information derived symbolically from another mode of perception.

This so-called 'wall,' disclosed in the pure mode of presentational immediacy, contributes itself to our experience only under the guise of spatial extension, combined with spatial perspective, and combined with sense-data which in this example reduce to colour alone.

I say that the wall contributes *itself* under this guise, in preference to saying that it contributes these universal characters in combination.   For the characters are combined by their exposition of one thing in a common world including ourselves, that one thing which I call the 'wall.'   Our perception is not confined to universal characters; we do not perceive disembodied colour or disembodied extensiveness: we perceive *the wall*'s colour and extensiveness.   The experienced fact is 'colour away on the wall for us.'   Thus the colour and the spatial perspective are abstract elements, characterizing the concrete way in which the wall enters into our experience.   They are therefore relational elements between the 'percipient at that moment,' and that other equally actual entity, or set of entities, which we call the 'wall at that moment.' But the mere colour and the mere spatial perspective are very abstract entities, because they are only arrived at by discarding the concrete relation-

ship between the wall-at-that-moment and the per-
cipient-at-that-moment. This concrete relationship
is a physical fact which may be very unessential to
the wall and very essential to the percipient. The
spatial relationship is equally essential both to wall
and percipient: but the colour side of the relationship is at that moment indifferent to the wall,
though it is part of the make-up of the percipient.
In this sense, and subject to their spatial relationship, contemporary events happen independently.
I call this type of experience 'presentational immediacy.' It expresses how contemporary events
are relevant to each other, and yet preserve a mutual independence. This relevance amid independence is the peculiar character of contemporane-
ousness. This presentational immediacy is only
of importance in high-grade organisms, and is a
physical fact which may, or may not, enter into
consciousness. Such entry will depend on attention and on the activity of conceptual functioning,
whereby physical experience and conceptual imagination are fused into knowledge.

9. *Perceptive Experience*

The word 'experience' is one of the most de-
ceitful in philosophy. Its adequate discussion

would be the topic for a treatise. I can only indicate those elements in my analysis of it which are relevant to the present train of thought.

Our experience, so far as it is primarily concerned with our direct recognition of a solid world of other things which are actual in the same sense that we are actual, has three main independent modes each contributing its share of components to our individual rise into one concrete moment of human experience. Two of these modes of experience I will call perceptive, and the third I will call the mode of conceptual analysis. In respect to pure perception, I call one of the two types concerned the mode of 'presentational immediacy,' and the other the mode of 'causal efficacy.' Both 'presentational immediacy' and 'causal efficacy' introduce into human experience components which are again analysable into actual things of the actual world and into abstract attributes, qualities, and relations, which express how those other actual things contribute themselves as components to our individual experience. These abstractions express how other actualities are component objects for us. I will therefore say that they 'objectify' for us the actual things in our 'environment.' Our most immediate environment is constituted by the various organs of our own bodies, our more remote environment is the physical world in the neighborhood. But the word 'environment' means those other actual things, which are 'objectified' in some important way so as to form component elements in our individual experience.

10. *Symbolic Reference in Perceptive Experience*

Of the two distinct perceptive modes, one mode 'objectifies' actual things under the guise of presentational immediacy, and the other mode, which I have not yet discussed, 'objectifies' them under the guise of causal efficacy. The synthetic activity whereby these two modes are fused into one perception is what I have called 'symbolic reference.' By symbolic reference the various actualities disclosed respectively by the two modes are either identified, or are at least correlated together as interrelated elements in our environment. Thus the result of symbolic reference is what the actual world is for us, as that datum in our experience productive of feelings, emotions, satisfactions, actions, and finally as the topic for conscious recognition when our mentality intervenes with its conceptual analysis. 'Direct recognition' is conscious recognition of a percept in a pure mode, devoid of symbolic reference.

Symbolic reference may be, in many respects, erroneous. By this I mean that some 'direct recognition' disagrees, in its report of the actual world, with the conscious recognition of the fused product resulting from symbolic reference. Thus error is primarily the product of symbolic reference, and not of conceptual analysis. Also symbolic reference itself is not primarily the outcome of conceptual analysis, though it is greatly promoted by it. For symbolic reference is still dominant in experience when such mental analysis is at a low ebb. We all know Aesop's fable of the dog who dropped a piece of meat to grasp at its reflection in the water. We must not, however, judge too severely of error. In the initial stages of mental progress, error in symbolic reference is the discipline which promotes imaginative freedom. Aesop's dog lost his meat, but he gained a step on the road towards a free imagination.

Thus symbolic reference must be explained antecedently to conceptual analysis, although there is a strong interplay between the two whereby they promote each other.

11. *Mental and Physical*

By way of being as intelligible as possible we
might tacitly assign symbolic reference to mental
activity, and thereby avoid some detailed explanation.   It is a matter of pure convention as to which
of our experiential activities we term mental and
which physical.   Personally I prefer to restrict
mentality to those experiential activities which include concepts in addition to percepts.   But much
of our perception is due to the enhanced subtlety
arising from a concurrent conceptual analysis.
Thus in fact there is no proper line to be drawn
between the physical and the mental constitution of
experience.   But there is no conscious knowledge
apart from the intervention of mentality in the
form of conceptual analysis.

It will be necessary later on to make some slight
reference to conceptual analysis; but at present I
must assume consciousness and its partial analysis
of experience, and return to the two modes of pure
perception.   The point that I want to make here
is, that the reason why low-grade purely physical
organisms cannot make mistakes is not primarily
their absence of thought, but their absence of presentational immediacy.   Aesop's dog, who was a

poor thinker, made a mistake by reason of an erroneous symbolic reference from presentational
immediacy to causal efficacy. In short, truth and
error dwell in the world by reason of synthesis:
every actual thing is synthetic: and symbolic reference is one primitive form of synthetic activity
whereby what is actual arises from its given
phases.

12. *Rôles of Sense-data and Space in
      Presentational Immediacy*

By 'presentational immediacy' I mean what is
usually termed 'sense-perception.' But I am using
the former term under limitations and extensions
which are foreign to the common use of the latter
term.

Presentational immediacy is our immediate perception of the contemporary external world, ap-
pearing as an element constitutive of our own experience. In this appearance the world discloses
itself to be a community of actual things, which
are actual in the same sense as we are.

This appearance is effected by the mediation of
qualities, such as colours, sounds, tastes, etc.,
which can with equal truth be described as our
sensations or as the qualities of the actual things

which we perceive. These qualities are thus relational between the perceiving subject and the
perceived things. They can be thus isolated only
by abstracting them from their implication in the
scheme of spatial relatedness of the perceived
things to each other and to the perceiving subject.
This relatedness of spatial extension is a complete
scheme, impartial between the observer and the
perceived things. It is the scheme of the morphol-
ogy of the complex organisms forming the community of the contemporary world. The way in
which each actual physical organism enters into
the make-up of its contemporaries has to conform
to this scheme. Thus the sense-data, such as colours, etc., or bodily feelings, introduce the extended physical entities into our experience under
perspectives provided by this spatial scheme. The
spatial relations by themselves are generic abstractions, and the sense-data are generic abstractions.
But the perspectives of the sense-data provided by
the spatial relations are the specific relations
whereby the external contemporary things are to
this extent part of our experience. These contemporary organisms, thus introduced as 'objects'
into experience, include the various organs of our
body, and the sense-data are then called bodily

feelings. The bodily organs, and those other external things which make important contributions to this mode of our perception, together form the contemporary environment of the percipient organism. The main facts about presentational immediacy are: (i) that the sense-data involved depend on the percipient organism and its spatial relations to the perceived organisms; (ii) that the contemporary world is exhibited as extended and as a plenum of organisms; (iii) that presentational immediacy is an important factor in the experience of only a few high-grade organisms, and that for the others it is embryonic or entirely negligible.

Thus the disclosure of a contemporary world by presentational immediacy is bound up with the disclosure of the solidarity of actual things by reason of their participation in an impartial system of spatial extension. Beyond this, the knowledge provided by pure presentational immediacy is vivid, precise, and barren. It is also to a large extent controllable at will. I mean that one moment of experience can predetermine to a considerable extent, by inhibitions, or by intensifications, or by other modifications, the characteristics of the presentational immediacy in succeeding moments of experience. This mode of perception, taken purely by itself, is barren, because we may not directly connect the qualitative presentations of other things with any intrinsic characters of those things. We see the image of a coloured chair, presenting to us the space behind a mirror; yet we thereby gain no knowledge concerning any intrinsic characters of spaces behind the mirror. But the image thus seen in a good mirror is just as much an immediate presentation of colour qualifying the world at a distance behind the mirror, as is our direct vision of the chair when we turn round and look at it. Pure presentational immediacy refuses to be divided into delusions and not-delusions. It is either all of it, or none of it, an immediate presentation of an external contemporary world as in its own right spatial. The sense-data involved in presentational immediacy have a wider relationship in the world than these contemporary things can express. In abstraction from this wider relationship, there is no means of determining the importance of the apparent qualification of contemporary objects by sense-data. For this reason the phrase 'mere appearance' carries the suggestion of barrenness. This wider relationship of the sense-data can only be understood by examining

the alternative mode of perception, the mode of
causal efficacy.   But in so far as contemporary
things are bound together by mere presentational
immediacy, they happen in complete independence
except for their spatial relations at the moment.
Also for most events, we presume that their intrinsic experience of presentational immediacy is so
embryonic as to be negligible.   This perceptive
mode is important only for a small minority of
elaborate organisms.

13. *Objectification*

In this explanation of Presentational Immediacy, I am conforming to the distinction according to which actual things are *objectively* in our
experience and *formally* existing in their own com-
pleteness.   I maintain that presentational immediacy is the peculiar way in which contemporary things are 'objectively' in our experience, and
that among the abstract entities which constitute
factors in the mode of introduction are those abstractions usually called sense-data:—for example,
colours,   sounds,   tastes,   touches,   and   bodily
feelings.

Thus 'objectification' itself is abstraction; since
no actual thing is 'objectified' in its 'formal' com-

pleteness. Abstraction expresses nature's mode of interaction and is not merely mental. When it abstracts, thought is merely conforming to nature —or rather, it is exhibiting itself as an element in nature. Synthesis and analysis require each other. Such a conception is paradoxical if you will persist in thinking of the actual world as a collection of passive actual substances with their private characters or qualities. In that case, it must be nonsense to ask, how one such substance can form a component in the make-up of another such substance. So long as this conception is retained, the difficulty is not relieved by calling each actual substance an event, or a pattern, or an occasion. The difficulty, which arises for such a conception, is to explain how the substances can be actually together in a sense derivative from that in which each individual substance is actual. But the conception of the world here adopted is that of functional activity. By this I mean that every actual thing is something by reason of its activity; whereby its nature consists in its relevance to other things, and its individuality consists in its synthesis of other things so far as they are relevant to it. In enquiring about any one individual we must ask how other individuals enter 'objectively' into the unity of its own experience. This unity of its own experience is that individual existing *formally*. We must also enquire how it enters into the 'formal' existence of other things; and this entrance is that individual existing *objectively*, that is to say—existing abstractly, exemplifying only some elements in its formal content.

With this conception of the world, in speaking of any actual individual, such as a human being, we must mean that man in one occasion of his experience. Such an occasion, or act, is complex and therefore capable of analysis into phases and other components. It is the most concrete actual entity, and the life of man from birth to death is a historic route of such occasions. These concrete moments are bound together into one society by a partial identity of form, and by the peculiarly full summation of its predecessors which each moment of the life-history gathers into itself. The man-at-one-moment concentrates in himself the colour of his own past, and he is the issue of it. The 'man in his whole life history' is an abstraction compared to the 'man in one such moment.' There are therefore three different meanings for the notion of a particular man,—Julius Cæsar, for example. The word 'Cæsar' may mean 'Cæsar in some one occasion of his existence': this is the most concrete of all the meanings. The word 'Cæsar' may mean 'the historic route of Cæsar's life from his Cæsarian birth to his Cæsarian assassination.' The word 'Cæsar' may mean 'the common form, or pattern, repeated in each occasion of Cæsar's life.' You may legitimately choose any one of these meanings; but when you have made your choice, you must in that context stick to it.

This doctrine of the nature of the life-history of an enduring organism holds for all types of organisms, which have attained to unity of experience, for electrons as well as for men. But mankind has gained a richness of experiential content denied to electrons. Whenever the 'all or none' principle holds, we are in some way dealing with one actual entity, and not with a society of such entities, nor with the analysis of components contributory to one such entity.

This lecture has maintained the doctrine of a direct experience of an external world. It is impossible fully to argue this thesis without getting too far away from my topic. I need only refer you to the first portion of Santayana's recent book, *Scepticism and Animal Faith*, for a conclusive

proof of the futile 'solipsism of the present moment'—or, in other words, utter scepticism—
which results from a denial of this assumption.
My second thesis, for which I cannot claim Santayana's authority, is that, if you consistently
maintain such direct individual experience, you will
be driven in your philosophical construction to a
conception of the world as an interplay of functional activity whereby each concrete individual
thing arises from its determinate relativity to the
settled world of other concrete individuals, at
least so far as the world is past and settled.

CHAPTER II

1. *Hume on Causal Efficacy*

It is the thesis of this work that human symbolism has its origin in the symbolic interplay between two distinct modes of direct perception of the external world. There are, in this way, two sources of information about the external world, closely connected but distinct. These modes do not repeat each other; and there is a real diversity of information. Where one is vague, the other is precise: where one is important, the other is trivial. But the two schemes of presentation have structural elements in common, which identify them as schemes of presentation of the same world. There are however gaps in the determination of the correspondence between the two morphologies. The schemes only partially intersect, and their true fusion is left indeterminate. The symbolic reference leads to a transference of emotion, purpose, and belief, which cannot be justified by an intellectual comparison of the direct information derived from the two schemes

30

and their elements of intersection. The justification, such as it is, must be sought in a pragmatic
appeal to the future. In this way intellectual criticism founded on subsequent experience can en-
large and purify the primitive naïve symbolic
transference.

I have termed one perceptive mode 'Presentational Immediacy,' and the other mode 'Causal
Efficacy.' In the previous lecture the mode of
presentational immediacy was discussed at length.
The present lecture must commence with the discussion of 'Causal Efficacy.' It will be evident to
you that I am here controverting the most cher-
ished tradition of modern philosophy, shared
alike by the school of empiricists which derives
from Hume, and the school of transcendental
idealists which derives from Kant. It is unnecessary to enter upon any prolonged justification of
this summary account of the tradition of modern
philosophy. But some quotations will summarize
neatly what is shared in common by the two types
of thought from which I am diverging. Hume *
writes:—"When both the objects are present to
the senses along with the relation, we call *this*
perception rather than reasoning; nor is there in

* *Treatise*, Part III, Section II.

this case any exercise of the thought, or any action, properly speaking, but a mere passive admission of the impressions through the organs of sensation. According to this way of thinking, we ought not to receive as reasoning any of the observations we may make concerning *identity* and the *relation* of *time* and *place*; since in none of them can the mind go beyond what is immediately present to the senses, either to discover the real existence or the relations of objects."

The whole force of this passage depends upon the tacit presupposition of the 'mind' as a passively receptive substance and of its 'impression' as forming its private world of accidents. There then remains nothing except the immediacy of these private attributes with their private relations which are also attributes of the mind. Hume explicitly repudiates this substantial view of mind.

But then, what is the force of the last clause of the last sentence, "since . . . objects"? The only reason for dismissing 'impressions' from having any demonstrative force in respect to 'the *real* existence or the relations of objects,' is the implicit notion that such impressions are mere private attributes of the mind. Santayana's book, *Scepticism and Animal Faith*, to which I have already referred, is in its earlier chapters a vigorous and thorough insistence, by every manner of beautiful illustration, that with Hume's premises there is no manner of escape from this dismissal of identity, time, and place from having any reference to a real world. There remains only what Santayana calls 'Solipsism of the Present Moment.' Even memory goes: for a memory-impression is not an impression of memory. It is only another immediate private impression.

It is unnecessary to cite Hume on Causation; for the preceding quotation carries with it his whole sceptical position. But a quotation * on substance is necessary to explain the ground of his explicit—as distinct from sporadic implicit presuppositions—doctrine on this point:—"I would fain ask those philosophers, who found so much of their reasonings on the distinction of substance and accident, and imagine we have clear ideas of each, whether the idea of substance be derived from the impressions of sensation or reflection? If it be conveyed to us by our senses, I ask, which of them, and after what manner? If it be perceived by the eyes, it must be a colour; if by the ears, a sound; if by the palate, a taste; and so of the other senses. But

* Cf. Hume's *Treatise*, Part I, Section VI.

I believe none will assert that substance is either
a colour, or sound, or a taste. The idea of substance must, therefore, be derived from an impression of reflection, if it really exist. But the
impressions of reflection resolve themselves into
our passions and emotions; none of which can pos-
sibly represent a substance. We have, therefore,
no idea of substance, distinct from that of a collection of particular qualities, nor have we any
other meaning when we either talk or reason concerning it."

This passage is concerned with a notion of
'substance,' which I do not entertain. Thus it
only indirectly controverts my position. I quote it
because it is the plainest example of Hume's initial
assumptions that (i) presentational immediacy,
and relations between presentationally immediate
entities, constitute the only type of perceptive experience, and that (ii) presentational immediacy
includes no demonstrative factors disclosing a contemporary world of extended actual things.

He discusses this question later in his *Treatise*
under the heading of the notion of 'Bodies'; and
arrives at analogous sceptical conclusions. These
conclusions rest upon an extraordinary naïve assumption of time as pure succession. The assump-

tion is naïve, because it is the natural thing to say; it is natural because it leaves out that characteristic of time which is so intimately interwoven that it is natural to omit it.

Time is known to us as the succession of our acts of experience, and thence derivatively as the succession of events objectively perceived in those acts. But this succession is not pure succession: it is the derivation of state from state, with the later state exhibiting conformity to the antecedent. Time in the concrete is the conformation of state to state, the later to the earlier; and the pure succession is an abstraction from the irreversible relationship of settled past to derivative present. The notion of pure succession is analogous to the notion of colour. There is no mere colour, but always some particular colour such as red or blue: analogously there is no pure succession, but always some particular relational ground in respect to which the terms succeed each other. The integers succeed each other in one way, and events succeed each other in another way; and, when we abstract from these ways of succession, we find that pure succession is an abstraction of the second order, a generic abstraction omitting the temporal character of time and the numerical relation of integers.

The past consists of the community of settled acts which, through their objectifications in the present act, establish the conditions to which that act must conform.

Aristotle conceived 'matter'—ὕλη—as being pure potentiality awaiting the incoming of form in order to become actual. Hence employing Aristotelian notions, we may say that the limitation of pure potentiality, established by 'objectifications' of the settled past, expresses that 'natural potentiality'—or, potentiality in nature—which is 'matter' with that basis of initial, realized form presupposed as the first phase in the self-creation of the present occasion. The notion of 'pure potentiality' here takes the place of Aristotle's 'matter,' and 'natural potentiality' is 'matter' with that given imposition of form from which each actual thing arises. All components which are *given* for experience are to be found in the analysis of natural potentiality. Thus the immediate present has to conform to what the past is for it, and the mere lapse of time is an abstraction from the more concrete relatedness of 'conformation.' The 'substantial' character of actual things is not primarily concerned with the predication of qualities. It expresses the stubborn fact that whatever is settled and actual must in due measure be conformed to by the self-creative activity. The phrase 'stubborn fact' exactly expresses the popular apprehension of this characteristic. Its primary phase, from which each actual thing arises, is the stubborn fact which underlies its existence. According to Hume there are no stubborn facts. Hume's doctrine may be good philosophy, but it is certainly not common sense. In other words, it fails before the final test of obvious verification.

2. *Kant and Causal Efficacy*

The school of transcendental idealists, derived from Kant, admit that causal efficacy is a factor in the phenomenal world; but hold that it does not belong to the sheer data presupposed in perception. It belongs to our ways of thought about the data. Our consciousness of the perceived world yields us an objective system, which is a fusion of mere data and modes of thought about those data.

The general Kantian reason for this position is that direct perception acquaints us with particular fact. Now particular fact is what simply occurs as particular datum. But we believe universal principles about all particular facts. Such universal knowledge cannot be derived from any selection of particular facts, each of which has just simply occurred. Thus our ineradicable belief is only explicable by reason of the doctrine that particular facts, as consciously apprehended, are the fusion of mere particular data with thought functioning according to categories which import their own universality in the modified data. Thus the phenomenal world, as in consciousness, is a complex of coherent judgments, framed according to fixed categories of thought, and with a content constituted by given data organized according to fixed forms of intuition.

This Kantian doctrine accepts Hume's naïve presupposition of 'simple occurrence' for the mere data. I have elsewhere called it the assumption of 'simple location,' by way of applying it to space as well as to time.

I directly deny this doctrine of 'simple occurrence.' There is nothing which 'simply happens.' Such a belief is the baseless doctrine of time as 'pure succession.' The alternative doctrine, that the pure succession of time is merely an abstract from the fundamental relationship of conformation, sweeps away the whole basis for the intervention of constitutive thought, or constitutive intuition, in the formation of the directly apprehended world. Universality of truth arises from the universality of relativity, whereby every particular actual thing lays upon the universe the obligation of conforming to it. Thus in the analysis of particular fact universal truths are discoverable, those truths expressing this obligation. The given-ness of experience—that is to say, all its data alike, whether general truths or particular sensa or presupposed forms of synthesis—expresses the specific character of the temporal relation of that act of experience to the settled actuality of the universe which is the source of all conditions. The fallacy of 'misplaced concreteness' abstracts from time this specific character, and leaves time with the mere generic character of pure succession.

3. *Direct Perception of Causal Efficacy*

The followers of Hume and the followers of Kant have thus their diverse, but allied, objections to the notion of any direct perception of causal efficacy, in the sense in which direct perception is antecedent to thought about it. Both schools find 'causal efficacy' to be the importation, into the data, of a way of thinking or judging about those data. One school calls it a habit of thought; the other school calls it a category of thought. Also for them the mere data are the pure sense-data.

If either Hume or Kant gives a proper account of the status of causal efficacy, we should find that our conscious apprehension of causal efficacy should depend to some extent on the vividness of the thought or of the pure intuitive discrimination of sense-data at the moment in question. For an apprehension which is the product of thought should sink in importance when thought is in the background. Also, according to this Humian–Kantian account, the thought in question is thought about the immediate sense-data. Accordingly a certain vividness of sense-data in immediate presentation should be favourable to apprehension of causal efficacy. For according to these accounts, causal efficacy is nothing else than a way of thinking about sense-data, given in presentational immediacy. Thus the inhibition of thought and the vagueness of sense-data should be extremely unfavourable to the prominence of causal efficacy as an element in experience.

The logical difficulties attending the direct perception of causal efficacy have been shown to depend on the sheer assumption that time is merely the generic notion of pure succession. This is an

instance of the fallacy of 'misplaced concreteness.'
Thus the way is now open to enquire empirically
whether in fact our apprehension of causal efficacy
does depend either on the vividness of sense-data
or on the activity of thought.

According to both schools, the importance of
causal efficacy, and of action exemplifying its presupposition, should be mainly characteristic of
high-grade organisms in their best moments. Now
if we confine attention to long-range identification
of cause and effect, depending on complex reasoning, undoubtedly such high-grade mentality and
such precise determination of sense-data are required. But each step in such reasoning depends
on the primary presupposition of the immediate
present moment conforming itself to the settled
environment of the immediate past. We must not
direct attention to the inferences from yesterday
to today, or even from five minutes ago to the immediate present. We must consider the immediate present in its relationship to the immediate
past. The overwhelming conformation of fact, in
present action, to antecedent settled fact is to be
found here.

My point is that this conformation of present
fact to immediate past is more prominent both in

apparent behaviour and in consciousness, when the organism is low grade. A flower turns to the light with much greater certainty than does a human being, and a stone conforms to the conditions set by its external environment with much greater certainty than does a flower. A dog anticipates the conformation of the immediate future to his present activity with the same certainty as a human being. When it comes to calculations and remote inferences, the dog fails. But the dog never acts as though the immediate future were irrelevant to the present. Irresolution in action arises from consciousness of a somewhat distant relevant future, combined with inability to evaluate its precise type. If we were not conscious of relevance, why is there irresolution in a sudden crisis?

Again a vivid enjoyment of immediate sense-data notoriously inhibits apprehension of the relevance of the future. The present moment is then all in all. In our consciousness it approximates to 'simple occurrence.'

Certain emotions, such as anger and terror, are apt to inhibit the apprehension of sense-data; but they wholly depend upon a vivid apprehension of the relevance of immediate past to the present, and of the present to the future. Again an inhibition

of familiar sense-data provokes the terrifying
sense of vague presences, effective for good or evil
over our fate.   Most living creatures, of daytime
habits, are more nervous in the dark, in the absence of the familiar visual sense-data.   But according to Hume, it is the very familiarity of the
sense-data which is required for causal inference.
Thus the sense of unseen effective presences in the
dark is the opposite of what should happen.

4.   *Primitiveness of Causal Efficacy*

The perception of conformation to realities in
the environment is the primitive element in our
external experience.   We conform to our bodily
organs and to the vague world which lies beyond
them.   Our primitive perception is that of 'conformation' vaguely, and of the yet vaguer relata
'oneself' and 'another' in the undiscriminated background.   Of course if relationships are unperceiv-
able, such a doctrine must be ruled out on theoretic
grounds.   But if we admit such perception, then
the perception of conformation has every mark of
a primitive element.   One part of our experience
is handy, and definite in our consciousness; also it
is easy to reproduce at will.   The other type of
experience, however insistent, is vague, haunting,
unmanageable.   The former type, for all its deco -

rative sense-experience, is barren. It displays a
world concealed under an adventitious show, a
show of our own bodily production. The latter
type is heavy with the contact of the things gone
by, which lay their grip on our immediate selves.
This latter type, the mode of causal efficacy, is the
experience dominating the primitive living organisms, which have a sense for the fate from which
they have emerged, and for the fate towards
which they go—the organisms which advance and
retreat but hardly differentiate any immediate dis-
play. It is a heavy, primitive experience. The
former type, the presentational immediacy, is the
superficial product of complexity, of subtlety; it
halts at the present, and indulges in a manageable self-enjoyment derived from the immediacy
of the show of things. Those periods in our lives
—when the perception of the pressure from a
world of things with characters in their own right,
characters mysteriously moulding our own natures,
becomes strongest—those periods are the product
of a reversion to some primitive state. Such a
reversion occurs when either some primitive functioning of the human organism is unusually height-
ened, or some considerable part of our habitual
sense-perception is unusually enfeebled.

Anger, hatred, fear, terror, attraction, love, hunger, eagerness, massive enjoyment, are feelings and emotions closely entwined with the primitive functioning of 'retreat from' and of 'expansion towards.' They arise in the higher organism as states due to a vivid apprehension that some such primitive mode of functioning is dominating the organism. But 'retreat from' and 'expansion towards,' divested of any detailed spatial discrimination, are merely reactions to the way externality is impressing on us its own character. You cannot retreat from mere subjectivity; for subjectivity is what we carry with us. Normally, we have almost negligible sense-presentations of the interior organs of our own bodies.

These primitive emotions are accompanied by the clearest recognition of other actual things reacting upon ourselves. The vulgar obviousness of such recognition is equal to the vulgar obviousness produced by the functioning of any one of our five senses. When we hate, it is a man that we hate and not a collection of sense-data—a causal, efficacious man. This primitive obviousness of the perception of 'conformation' is illustrated by the emphasis on the pragmatic aspect of occurrences, which is so prominent in modern philosophical thought. There can be no useful aspect of anything unless we admit the principle of conformation, whereby what is already made becomes a determinant of what is in the making. The obviousness of the pragmatic aspect is simply the obviousness of the perception of the fact of conformation.

In practice we never doubt the fact of the conformation of the present to the immediate past. It belongs to the ultimate texture of experience, with the same evidence as does presentational immediacy. The present fact is luminously the outcome from its predecessors, one quarter of a second ago. Unsuspected factors may have intervened; dynamite may have exploded. But, however that may be, the present event issues subject to the limitations laid upon it by the actual nature of the immediate past. If dynamite explodes, then present fact is that issue from the past which is consistent with dynamite exploding. Further, we unhesitatingly argue backwards to the inference, that the complete analysis of the past must disclose in it those factors which provide the conditions for the present. If dynamite be now exploding, then in the immediate past there was a charge of dynamite unexploded.

The fact that our consciousness is confined to

an analysis of experience in the present is no difficulty. For the theory of the universal relativity
of actual individual things leads to the distinction
between the present moment of experience, which
is the sole datum for conscious analysis, and perception of the contemporary world, which is the
only one factor in this datum.

The contrast between the comparative emptiness of Presentational Immediacy and the deep
significance disclosed by Causal Efficacy is at the
root of the pathos which haunts the world.

'Pereunt et imputantur'

is the inscription on old sundials in 'religious'
houses:

'The hours perish and are laid to account.'

Here 'Pereunt' refers to the world disclosed in
immediate presentation, gay with a thousand tints,
passing, and intrinsically meaningless. 'Imputantur' refers to the world disclosed in its causal efficacy, where each event infects the ages to come,
for good or for evil, with its own individuality.
Almost all pathos includes a reference to lapse of
time.

The final stanza of Keats' *Eve of St. Agnes*
commences with the haunting lines:—

'And they are gone: ay, ages long ago
   Those lovers fled away into the storm.'

There the pathos of the lapse of time arises from
the imagined fusion of the two perceptive modes
by one intensity of emotion. Shakespeare, in the
springtime of the modern world, fuses the two
elements by exhibiting the infectiousness of gay
immediacy:—

'. . . daffodils,
  That come before the swallow dares, and take
  The winds of March with beauty; . . .'
    (*The Winter's Tale*, iv, iv, 118–120).

But sometimes men are overstrained by their un-
divided attention to the causal elements in the nature of things. Then in some tired moment there
comes a sudden relaxation, and the mere presentational side of the world overwhelms with the
sense of its emptiness. As William Pitt, the Prime
Minister of England through the darkest period
of the French Revolutionary wars, lay on his
death-bed at England's worst moment in that
struggle, he was heard to murmur.

'What shades we are, what shadows we pursue!'
His mind had suddenly lost the sense of causal efficacy, and was illuminated by the remembrance of

the intensity of emotion, which had enveloped his life, in its comparison with the barren emptiness of the world passing in sense-presentation.

The world, given in sense-presentation, is not the aboriginal experience of the lower organisms, later to be sophisticated by the inference to causal efficacy. The contrary is the case. First the causal side of experience is dominating, then the sense-presentation gains in subtlety. Their mutual symbolic reference is finally purged by consciousness and the critical reason with the aid of a pragmatic appeal to consequences.

5. *The Intersection of the Modes of Perception*

There cannot be symbolic reference between percepts derived from one mode and percepts from the other mode, unless in some way these percepts intersect. By this 'intersection' I mean that a pair of such percepts must have elements of structure in common, whereby they are marked out for the action of symbolic reference.

There are two elements of common structure, which can be shared in common by a percept derived from presentational immediacy and by another derived from causal efficacy. These elements are (1) sense-data, and (2) locality.

The sense-data are 'given' for presentational immediacy. This given-ness of the sense-data, as the basis of this perceptive mode, is the great doctrine common to Hume and Kant. But what is already given for experience can only be derived from that natural potentiality which shapes a particular experience in the guise of causal efficacy. Causal efficacy is the hand of the settled past in the formation of the present. The sense-data must therefore play a double rôle in perception. In the mode of presentational immediacy they are projected to exhibit the contemporary world in its spatial relations. In the mode of causal efficacy they exhibit the almost instantaneously precedent bodily organs as imposing their characters on the experience in question. We see the picture, and we see it with our eyes; we touch the wood, and we touch it with our hands; we smell the rose, and we smell it with our nose; we hear the bell, and we hear it with our ears; we taste the sugar, and we taste it with our palate. In the case of bodily feelings the two locations are identical. The foot both is giving pain and is the seat of the pain. Hume himself tacitly asserts this double reference in the second of the quotations previously made. He writes: "If it be perceived by the eyes, it must be a colour; if by the ears, a sound; if by the palate, a taste; and so of the other senses." Thus in asserting the lack of perception of causality, he implicitly presupposes it. For what is the meaning of '*by*' in '*by* the eyes,' '*by* the ears,' '*by* the palate'? His argument presupposes that sense-data, functioning in presentational immediacy, are 'given' by reason of 'eyes,' 'ears,' 'palates' functioning in causal efficacy. Otherwise his argument is involved in a vicious regress. For it must begin again over eyes, ears, palates; also it must explain the meaning of 'by' and 'must' in a sense which does not destroy his argument.

This double reference is the basis of the whole physiological doctrine of perception. The details of this doctrine are, in this discussion, philosophically irrelevant. Hume with the clarity of genius states the fundamental point, that sense-data functioning in an act of experience demonstrate that they are given *by* the causal efficacy of actual bodily organs. He refers to this causal efficacy as a component in direct perception. Hume's argument first tacitly presupposes the two modes of perception, and then tacitly assumes that presentational immediacy is the only mode. Also Hume's followers in developing his doctrine presuppose

that presentational immediacy is primitive, and
that causal efficacy is the sophisticated derivative.
This is a complete inversion of the evidence. So
far as Hume's own teaching is concerned, there is,
of course, another alternative: it is that Hume's
disciples have misinterpreted Hume's final position. On this hypothesis, his final appeal to 'practice' is an appeal against the adequacy of the then
current metaphysical categories as interpretive of
obvious experience. This theory about Hume's
own beliefs is in my opinion improbable: but,
apart from Hume's own estimate of his philosophical achievement, it is in this sense that we
must reverence him as one of the greatest of
philosophers.

The conclusion of this argument is that the intervention of any sense-datum in the actual world
cannot be expressed in any simple way, such as
mere qualification of a region of space, or alter-
natively as the mere qualification of a state of
mind. The sense-data, required for immediate
sense-perception, enter into experience in virtue of
the efficacy of the environment. This environment
includes the bodily organs. For example, in the
case of hearing sound the physical waves have
entered the ears, and the agitations of the nerves

have excited the brain. The sound is then heard as coming from a certain region in the external world. Thus perception in the mode of causal efficacy discloses that the data in the mode of sense-perception are provided by it. This is the reason why there are such given elements. Every such datum constitutes a link between the two perceptive modes. Each such link, or datum, has a complex ingression into experience, requiring a reference to the two perceptive modes. These sense-data can be conceived as constituting the character of a many-termed relationship between the organisms of the past environment and those of the contemporary world.

6. *Localization*

The partial community of structure, whereby the two perceptive modes yield immediate demonstration of a common world, arises from their reference of sense-data, common to both, to localizations, diverse or identical, in a spatio-temporal system common to both. For example, colour is referred to an external space and to the eyes as organs of vision. In so far as we are dealing with one or other of these pure perceptive modes, such reference is direct demonstration; and, as isolated in conscious analysis, is ultimate fact against which there is no appeal. Such isolation, or at least some approach to it, is fairly easy in the case of presentational immediacy, but is very difficult in the case of causal efficacy. Complete ideal purity of perceptive experience, devoid of any symbolic reference, is in practice unobtainable for either perceptive mode.

Our judgments on causal efficacy are almost inextricably warped by the acceptance of the symbolic reference between the two modes as the completion of our direct knowledge. This acceptance is not merely in thought, but also in action, emotion, and purpose, all precedent to thought. This symbolic reference is a datum for thought in its analysis of experience. By trusting this datum, our conceptual scheme of the universe is in general logically coherent with itself, and is correspondent to the ultimate facts of the pure perceptive modes. But occasionally, either the coherence or the verification fails. We then revise our conceptual scheme so as to preserve the general trust in the symbolic reference, while relegating definite details of that reference to the category of errors. Such errors are termed 'delusive appearances.' This error arises from the extreme vagueness of the spatial and temporal perspectives in the case of perception in the pure mode of causal efficacy. There is no adequate definition of localization, so far as what emerges into analytic consciousness. The principle of relativity leads us to hold that, with adequate conscious analysis, such local relationships leave their faint impress in experience. But in general such detailed analysis is far beyond the capacity of human consciousness.

So far as concerns the causal efficacy of the world external to the human body, there is the most insistent perception of a circumambient efficacious world of beings. But exact discrimination of thing from thing, and of position from position, is extremely vague, almost negligible. The definite discrimination, which in fact we do make, arises almost wholly by reason of symbolic reference from presentational immediacy. The case is different in respect to the human body. There is still vagueness in comparison with the accurate definition of immediate presentation; although the locality of various bodily organs which are efficacious in the regulation of the sense-data, and of the feelings, are fairly well-defined in the pure perceptive mode of causal efficacy. The symbolic transference of course intensifies the definition. But, apart from such transference, there is some adequacy of definite demarcation.

Thus in the intersection of the two modes, the spatial and temporal relationships of the human body, as causally apprehended, to the external contemporary world, as immediately presented, afford a fairly definite scheme of spatial and temporal reference whereby we test the symbolic use of sense-projection for the determination of the positions of bodies controlling the course of nature. Ultimately all observation, scientific or popular, consists in the determination of the spatial relation of the bodily organs of the observer to the location of 'projected' sense-data.

7. *The Contrast Between Accurate Definition and Importance*

The reason why the projected sense-data are in general used as symbol, is that they are handy, definite, and manageable. We can see, or not see, as we like: we can hear, or not hear. There are limits to this handiness of the sense-data: but they are emphatically the manageable elements in our perceptions of the world. The sense of control-

ling presences has the contrary character: it is unmanageable, vague, and ill-defined.

But for all their vagueness, for all their lack of
definition, these controlling presences, these
sources of power, these things with an inner life,
with their own richness of content, these beings,
with the destiny of the world hidden in their natures, are what we want to know about. As we
cross a road busy with traffic, we see the colour
of the cars, their shapes, the gay colours of their
occupants; but at the moment we are absorbed in
using this immediate show as a symbol for the
forces determining the immediate future.

We enjoy the symbol, but we also penetrate to
the meaning. The symbols do not create their
meaning: the meaning, in the form of actual effective beings reacting upon us, exists for us in its
own right. But the symbols discover this meaning
for us. They discover it because, in the long
course of adaptation of living organisms to their
environment, nature * taught their use. It developed us so that our projected sensations indicate
in general those regions which are the seat of important organisms.

* Cf. *Prolegomena to an Idealist Theory of Knowledge*, by
Norman Kemp Smith (London: Macmillan, 1924).

Our relationships to these bodies are precisely our reactions to them. The projection of our sensations is nothing else than the illustration of the world in partial accordance with the systematic scheme, in space and in time, to which these reactions conform.

The bonds of causal efficacy arise from without us. They disclose the character of the world from which we issue, an inescapable condition round which we shape ourselves. The bonds of presentational immediacy arise from within us, and are subject to intensifications and inhibitions and diversions according as we accept their challenge or reject it. The sense-data are not properly to be termed 'mere impressions'—except so far as any technical term will do. They also represent the conditions arising out of the active perceptive functioning as conditioned by our own natures. But our natures must conform to the causal efficacy. Thus the causal efficacy *from* the past is at least one factor giving our presentational immediacy *in* the present. The *how* of our present experience must conform to the *what* of the past in us.

Our experience arises out of the past: it enriches with emotion and purpose its presentation of the contemporary world: and it bequeaths its character to the future, in the guise of an effective element forever adding to, or subtracting from, the richness of the world.   For good or for evil,

'Pereunt et imputantur.'

8. *Conclusion*

In this chapter, and in the former chapter, the general character of symbolism has been discussed. It plays a dominant part in the way in which all higher organisms conduct their lives.   It is the cause of progress, and the cause of error.   The higher animals have gained a faculty of great power, by means of which they can define with some accuracy those distant features in the immediate world by which their future lives are to be determined.   But this faculty is not infallible; and the risks are commensurate with its importance.   It is the purpose of the next chapter to illustrate this doctrine by an analysis of the part played by this habit of symbolism in promoting the cohesion, the progress, and the dissolution of human societies.

CHAPTER III

Uses of Symbolism

The attitude of mankind towards symbolism exhibits an unstable mixture of attraction and repulsion. The practical intelligence, the theoretical desire to pierce to ultimate fact, and ironic critical impulses have contributed the chief motives towards the repulsion from symbolism. Hard-headed men want facts and not symbols. A clear theoretic intellect, with its generous enthusiasm for the exact truth at all costs and hazards, pushes aside symbols as being mere make-believes, veiling and distorting that inner sanctuary of simple truth which reason claims as its own. The ironic critics of the follies of humanity have performed notable service in clearing away the lumber of useless ceremony symbolizing the degrading fancies of a savage past. The repulsion from symbolism stands out as a well-marked element in the cultural history of civilized people. There can be no reasonable doubt but that this contin-

uous criticism has performed a necessary service
in the promotion of a wholesome civilization,
both on the side of the practical efficiency of organized society, and on the side of a robust direction of thought.

No account of the uses of symbolism is complete without this recognition that the symbolic
elements in life have a tendency to run wild, like
the vegetation in a tropical forest. The life of
humanity can easily be overwhelmed by its symbolic accessories. A continuous process of prun-
ing, and of adaptation to a future ever requiring
new forms of expression, is a necessary function
in every society. The successful adaptation of
old symbols to changes of social structure is the
final mark of wisdom in sociological statesman-
ship. Also an occasional revolution in symbolism is required.

There is, however, a Latin proverb upon which,
in our youth, some of us have been set to write
themes. In English it reads thus:—Nature, ex-
pelled with a pitchfork, ever returns. This proverb is exemplified by the history of symbolism.
However you may endeavour to expel it, it ever
returns. Symbolism is no mere idle fancy or cor-
rupt degeneration: it is inherent in the very tex-

ture of human life. Language itself is a symbolism. And, as another example, however you reduce the functions of your government to their utmost simplicity, yet symbolism remains. It may be a healthier, manlier ceremonial, suggesting finer notions. But still it is symbolism. You abolish the etiquette of a royal court, with its suggestion of personal subordination, but at official receptions you ceremonially shake the hand of the Governor of your State. Just as the feudal doctrine of a subordination of classes, reaching up to the ultimate overlord, requires its symbolism; so does the doctrine of human equality obtain its symbolism. Mankind, it seems, has to find a symbol in order to express itself. Indeed 'expression' is 'symbolism.'

When the public ceremonial of the State has been reduced to the barest simplicity, private clubs and associations at once commence to reconstitute symbolic actions. It seems as though mankind must always be masquerading. This imperative impulse suggests that the notion of an idle masquerade is the wrong way of thought about the symbolic elements in life. The function of these elements is to be definite, manageable, reproducible, and also to be charged with their own emotional efficacity: symbolic transference invests their correlative meanings with some or all of these attributes of the symbols, and thereby lifts the meanings into an intensity of definite effectiveness—as elements in knowledge, emotion, and purpose,—an effectiveness which the meanings may, or may not, deserve on their own account. The object of symbolism is the enhancement of the importance of what is symbolized.

In a discussion of instances of symbolism, our first difficulty is to discover exactly what is being symbolized. The symbols are specific enough, but it is often extremely difficult to analyse what lies beyond them, even though there is evidently some strong appeal beyond the mere ceremonial acts.

It seems probable that in any ceremonial which has lasted through many epochs, the symbolic interpretation, so far as we can obtain it, varies much more rapidly than does the actual ceremonial. Also in its flux a symbol will have different meanings for different people. At any epoch some people have the dominant mentality of the past, some of the present, others of the future, and others of the many problematic futures which will never dawn. For these various groups an old symbolism will have different shades of vague meaning.

In order to appreciate the necessary function of symbolism in the life of any society of human beings we must form some estimate of the binding and disruptive forces at work. There are many varieties of human society, each requiring its own particular investigation so far as details are concerned. We will fix attention on nations, occupying definite countries. Thus geographical unity is at once presupposed. Communities with geographical unity constitute the primary type of communities which we find in the world. Indeed the lower we go in the scale of being, the more necessary is geographical unity for that close interaction of individuals which constitutes society. Societies of the higher animals, of insects, of molecules, all possess geographical unity. A rock is nothing else than a society of molecules, indulging in every species of activity open to molecules. I draw attention to this lowly form of society in order to dispel the notion that social life is a peculiarity of the higher organisms. The contrary is the case. So far as survival value is concerned, a piece of rock, with its past history of some eight hundred millions of years, far outstrips the short

span attained by any nation. The emergence of
life is better conceived as a bid for freedom on
the part of organisms, a bid for a certain independence of individuality with self-interests and
activities not to be construed purely in terms of
environmental obligations. The immediate effect of this emergence of sensitive individuality
has been to reduce the term of life for societies
from hundreds of millions of years to hundreds
of years, or even to scores of years.

The emergence of living beings cannot be as-
cribed to the superior survival value either of the
individuals, or of their societies. National life
has to face the disruptive elements introduced by
these extreme claims for individual idiosyncrasies.
We require both the advantages of social preservation, and the contrary stimulus of the hetero-
geneity derived from freedom. The society is to
run smoothly amidst the divergencies of its individuals. There is a revolt from the mere causal
obligations laid upon individuals by the social
character of the environment. This revolt first
takes the form of blind emotional impulse; and
later, in civilized societies, these impulses are crit-
icized and deflected by reason. In any case, there
are individual springs of action which escape from

the obligations of social conformity. In order to replace this decay of secure instinctive response, various intricate forms of symbolic expression of the various purposes of social life have been introduced. The response to the symbol is almost automatic but not quite; the reference to the meaning is there, either for additional emotional support, or for criticism. But the reference is not so clear as to be imperative. The imperative instinctive conformation to the influence of the environment has been modified. Something has replaced it, which by its superficial character invites criticism, and by its habitual use generally escapes it. Such symbolism makes connected thought possible by expressing it, while at the same time it automatically directs action. In the place of the force of instinct which suppresses individuality, society has gained the efficacy of symbols, at once preservative of the commonweal and of the individual standpoint.

Among the particular kinds of symbolism which serve this purpose, we must place first Language. I do not mean language in its function of a bare indication of abstract ideas, or of particular actual things, but language clothed with its complete influence for the nation in question. In ad-

dition to its bare indication of meaning, words
and phrases carry with them an enveloping sug-
gestiveness and an emotional efficacy. This function of language depends on the way it has been
used, on the proportionate familiarity of particular phrases, and on the emotional history associated with their meanings and thence derivatively
transferred to the phrases themselves. If two
nations speak the same language, this emotional
efficacy of words and phrases will in general differ
for the two. What is familiar for one nation
will be strange for the other nation; what is
charged with intimate associations for the one is
comparatively empty for the other. For example,
if the two nations are somewhat widely sundered,
with a different fauna and flora, the nature-poetry
of one nation will lack its complete directness of
appeal to the other nation—compare Walt Whit-
man's phrase,

'The wide unconscious scenery of my land'
for an American, with Shakespeare's

'. . . this little world,
This precious stone set in the silver sea,'
for an Englishman. Of course anyone, American
or English, with the slightest sense for history
and kinship, or with the slightest sympathetic

imagination, can penetrate to the feelings conveyed by both phrases. But the direct first-hand intuition, derived from earliest childhood memories, is for the one nation that of continental width, and for the other nation that of the little island world. Now the love of the sheer geographical aspects of one's country, of its hills, its mountains, and its plains, of its trees, its flowers, its birds, and its whole nature-life, is no small element in that binding force which makes a nation. It is the function of language, working through literature and through the habitual phrases of early life, to foster this diffused feeling of the common possession of a treasure infinitely precious.

I must not be misunderstood to mean that this example has any unique importance. It is only one example of what can be illustrated in a hundred ways. Also language is not the only symbolism effective for this purpose. But in an especial manner, language binds a nation together by the common emotions which it elicits, and is yet the instrument whereby freedom of thought and of individual criticism finds its expression.

My main thesis is that a social system is kept together by the blind force of instinctive actions, and of instinctive emotions clustered around habits and prejudices. It is therefore not true that any advance in the scale of culture inevitably tends to the preservation of society. On the whole, the contrary is more often the case, and any survey of nature confirms this conclusion. A new element in life renders in many ways the operation of the old instincts unsuitable. But unexpressed instincts are unanalysed and blindly felt. Disruptive forces, introduced by a higher level of existence, are then warring in the dark against an invisible enemy. There is no foothold for the intervention of 'rational consideration'—to use Henry Osborn Taylor's admirable phrase. The symbolic expression of instinctive forces drags them out into the open: it differentiates them and delineates them. There is then opportunity for reason to effect, with comparative speed, what otherwise must be left to the slow operation of the centuries amid ruin and reconstruction. Mankind misses its opportunities, and its failures are a fair target for ironic criticism. But the fact that reason too often fails does not give fair ground for the hysterical conclusion that it never succeeds. Reason can be compared to the force of gravitation, the weakest of all natural forces, but in the end the creator of suns and of stellar systems:—those great societies of the Universe. Symbolic expression first preserves society by adding emotion to instinct, and secondly it affords a foothold for reason by its delineation of the particular instinct which it expresses. This doctrine of the disruptive tendency due to novelties, even those involving a rise to finer levels, is illustrated by the effect of Christianity on the stability of the Roman Empire. It is also illustrated by the three revolutions which secured liberty and equality for the world—namely the English revolutionary period of the seventeenth century, the American Revolution, and the French Revolution. England barely escaped a disruption of its social system; America was never in any such danger; France, where the entrance of novelty was most intense, did for a time experience this collapse. Edmund Burke, the Whig statesman of the eighteenth century, was the philosopher who was the approving prophet of the two earlier revolutions, and the denunciatory prophet of the French Revolution. A man of genius and a statesman, who has immediately observed two revolutions, and has meditated deeply on a third, deserves to be heard when he speaks on the forces which bind and disrupt societies. Unfortunately statesmen are swayed by the passions of the moment, and Burke shared this defect to the full, so as to be carried away by the reactionary passions aroused by the French Revolution. Thus the wisdom of his general conception of social forces is smothered by the wild unbalanced conclusions which he drew from them: his greatness is best shown by his attitude towards the American Revolution. His more general reflections are contained first, in his youthful work *A Vindication of Natural Society*, and secondly, in his *Reflections on the French Revolution.*. The earlier work was meant ironically; but, as is often the case with genius, he prophesied unknowingly. This essay is practically written round the thesis that advances in the art of civilization are apt to be destructive of the social system. Burke conceived this conclusion to be a *reductio ad absurdum*. But it is the truth. The second work—a work which in its immediate effect was perhaps the most harmful ever written —directs attention to the importance of 'prejudice' as a binding social force. There again I hold that he was right in his premises and wrong in his conclusions.

Burke surveys the standing miracle of the existence of an organised society, culminating in the smooth unified action of the state. Such a society may consist of millions of individuals, each with its individual character, its individual aims, and its individual selfishness. He asks what is the force which leads this throng of separate units to coöperate in the maintenance of an organised state, in which each individual has his part to play—political, economic, and æsthetic. He contrasts the complexity of the functionings of a civilised society with the sheer diversities of its individual citizens considered as a mere group or crowd. His answer to the riddle is that the magnetic force is 'prejudice,' or in other words, 'use and wont.' Here he anticipates the whole modern theory of 'herd psychology,' and at the same time deserts the fundamental doctrine of the Whig party, as formed in the seventeenth century and sanctioned by Locke. This conventional Whig doctrine was that the state derived its origin from an 'original contract' whereby the mere crowd voluntarily organised itself into a society. Such a doctrine seeks the origin of the state in a baseless historical fiction. Burke was well ahead of his time in drawing attention to the importance of precedence as a political force. Unfortu-

nately, in the excitement of the moment, Burke
construed the importance of precedence as im-
plying the negation of progressive reform.

Now, when we examine how a society bends its
individual members to function in conformity
with its needs, we discover that one important op-
erative agency is our vast system of inherited
symbolism. There is an intricate expressed symbolism of language and of act, which is spread
throughout the community, and which evokes
fluctuating apprehension of the basis of common
purposes. The particular direction of individual
action is directly correlated to the particular
sharply defined symbols presented to him at the
moment. The response of action to symbol may
be so direct as to cut out any effective reference
to the ultimate thing symbolized. This elimina-
tion of meaning is termed reflex action. Sometimes there does intervene some effective reference to the meaning of the symbol. But this
meaning is not recalled with the particularity and
definiteness which would yield any rational enlight-
enment as to the specific action required to secure
the final end. The meaning is vague but insistent.
Its insistence plays the part of hypnotizing the
individual to complete the specific action associ-

ated with the symbol. In the whole transaction, the elements which are clear-cut and definite are the specific symbols and the actions which should issue from the symbols. But in themselves the symbols are barren facts whose direct associative force would be insufficient to procure automatic conformity. There is not sufficient repetition, or sufficient similarity of diverse occasions, to secure mere automatic obedience. But in fact the symbol evokes loyalties to vaguely conceived notions, fundamental for our spiritual natures. The result is that our natures are stirred to suspend all antagonistic impulses, so that the symbol procures its required response in action. Thus the social symbolism has a double meaning. It means pragmatically the direction of individuals to specific actions; and it also means theoretically the vague ultimate reasons with their emotional accompaniments, whereby the symbols acquire their power to organize the miscellaneous crowd into a smoothly running community.

The contrast between a state and an army illustrates this principle. A state deals with a greater complexity of situation than does its army. In this sense it is a looser organization, and in regard to the greater part of its population the

communal symbolism cannot rely for its effectiveness on the frequent recurrence of almost identical
situations.   But a disciplined regiment is trained
to act as a unit in a definite set of situations.   The
bulk of human life escapes from the reach of this
military discipline.   The regiment is drilled for
one species of job.   The result is that there is
more reliance on automatism, and less reliance
on the appeal to ultimate reasons.   The trained
soldier acts automatically on receiving the word
of command.   He responds to the sound and cuts
out the idea; this is reflex action.   But the appeal
to the deeper side is still important in an army;
although it is provided for in another set of symbols, such as the flag, and the memorials of the
honourable service of the regiment, and other
symbolic appeals to patriotism.   Thus in an army
there is one set of symbols to produce automatic
obedience in a limited set of circumstances, and
there is another set of symbols to produce a general sense of the importance of the duties performed.   This second set prevents random reflection from sapping automatic response to the
former set.

For the greater number of citizens of a state
there is in practice no reliable automatic obedi-

ence to any symbol such as the word of command for soldiers, except in a few instances such as the response to the signals of the traffic police. Thus the state depends in a very particular way upon the prevalence of symbols which combine direction to some well-known course of action with some deeper reference to the purpose of the state. The self-organisation of society depends on commonly diffused symbols evoking commonly diffused ideas, and at the same time indicating commonly understood actions. Usual forms of verbal expression are the most important example of such symbolism. Also the heroic aspect of the history of the country is the symbol for its immediate worth.

When a revolution has sufficiently destroyed this common symbolism leading to common actions for usual purposes, society can only save itself from dissolution by means of a reign of terror. Those revolutions which escape a reign of terror have left intact the fundamental efficient symbolism of society. For example, the English revolutions of the seventeenth century and the American revolution of the eighteenth century left the ordinary life of their respective communities nearly unchanged. When George Washing-

ton had replaced George III, and Congress had
replaced the English Parliament, Americans were
still carrying on a well-understood system so far
as the general structure of their social life was
concerned. Life in Virginia must have assumed
no very different aspect from that which it had
exhibited before the revolution. In Burke's
phraseology, the prejudices on which Virginian
society depended were unbroken. The ordinary
signs still beckoned people to their ordinary actions, and suggested the ordinary common-sense
justification.

One difficulty of explaining my meaning is that
the intimate effective symbolism consists of the
various types of expression which permeate society and evoke a sense of common purpose. No
one detail is of much importance. The whole
range of symbolic expression is required. A national hero, such as George Washington or Jef-
ferson, is a symbol of the common purpose which
animates American life. This symbolic function
of great men is one of the difficulties in obtaining
a balanced historical judgment. There is the
hysteria of depreciation, and there is the opposite hysteria which dehumanises in order to exalt.
It is very difficult to exhibit the greatness without

losing the human being. Yet we know that at least *we* are human beings; and half the inspiration of our heroes is lost when we forget that *they* were human beings.

I mention great Americans, because I am speaking in America. But exactly the same truth holds for the great men of all countries and ages.

The doctrine of symbolism developed in these lectures enables us to distinguish between pure instinctive action, reflex action, and symbolically conditioned action. Pure instinctive action is that functioning of an organism which is wholly analysable in terms of those conditions laid upon its development by the settled facts of its external environment, conditions describable without any reference to its perceptive mode of presentational immediacy. This pure instinct is the response of an organism to pure causal efficacy.

According to this definition, pure instinct is the most primitive type of response which is yielded by organisms to the stimulus of their environment. All physical response on the part of inorganic matter to its environment is thus properly to be termed instinct. In the case of organic matter, its primary difference from inorganic nature is its greater delicacy of internal mutual adjustment of minute parts and, in some cases, its emotional enhancement. Thus instinct, or this immediate adjustment to immediate environment, becomes more prominent in its function of directing action for the purposes of the living organism. The world is a community of organisms; these organisms in the mass determine the environmental influence on any one of them; there can only be a persistent community of persistent organisms when the environmental influence in the shape of instinct is favourable to the survival of the individuals. Thus the community as an environment is responsible for the survival of the separate individuals which compose it; and these separate individuals are responsible for their contributions to the environment. Electrons and molecules survive because they satisfy this primary law for a stable order of nature in connection with given societies of organisms.

Reflex action is a relapse towards a more complex type of instinct on the part of organisms which enjoy, or have enjoyed, symbolically conditioned action. Thus its discussion must be postponed. Symbolically conditioned action arises in the higher organisms which enjoy the perceptive mode of presentational immediacy, that is to say, sense-presentation of the contemporary world. This sense-presentation symbolically promotes an analysis of the massive perception of causal efficacy. The causal efficacy is thereby perceived as analysed into components with the locations in space primarily belonging to the sense-presentations. In the case of perceived organisms external to the human body, the spatial discrimination involved in the human perception of their pure causal efficacy is so feeble, that practically there is no check on this symbolic transference, apart from the indirect check of pragmatic consequences, —in other words, either survival-value, or self-satisfaction, logical and æsthetic.

Symbolically conditioned action is action which is thus conditioned by the analysis of the perceptive mode of causal efficacy effected by symbolic transference from the perceptive mode of presentational immediacy. This analysis may be right or wrong, according as it does, or does not, conform to the actual distribution of the efficacious bodies. In so far as it is sufficiently correct under normal circumstances, it enables an organism to conform its actions to long-ranged analysis of the particular circumstances of its environment. So far as this type of action prevails, pure instinct is

superseded. This type of action is greatly promoted by thought, which uses the symbols as ref-
erent to their meanings. There is no sense in
which pure instinct can be wrong. But symbolically conditioned action can be wrong, in the sense
that it may arise from a false symbolic analysis
of causal efficacy.

Reflex action is that organic functioning which
is wholly dependent on sense-presentation, unac-
companied by any analysis of causal efficacy *via*
symbolic reference. The conscious analysis of
perception is primarily concerned with the analysis of the symbolic relationship between the two
perceptive modes. Thus reflex action is hindered
by thought, which inevitably promotes the prominence of symbolic reference.

Reflex action arises when by the operation of
symbolism the organism has acquired the habit of
action in response to immediate sense-perception,
and has discarded the symbolic enhancement of
causal efficacy. It thus represents the relapse
from the high-grade activity of symbolic reference. This relapse is practically inevitable in the
absence of conscious attention. Reflex action cannot in any sense be said to be wrong, though it
may be unfortunate.

Thus the important binding factor in a community of insects probably falls under the notion of pure instinct, as here defined. For each individual insect is probably such an organism that the causal conditions which it inherits from the immediate past are adequate to determine its social actions. But reflex action plays its subordinate part. For the sense-perceptions of the insects have in certain fields of action assumed an automatic determination of the insects' activities. Still more feebly, symbolically conditioned action intervenes for such situations when the sense-presentation provides a symbolically defined specification of the causal situation. But only active thought can save symbolically conditioned action from quickly relapsing into reflex action. The most successful examples of community life exist when pure instinct reigns supreme. These examples occur only in the inorganic world; among societies of active molecules forming rocks, planets, solar systems, star clusters.

The more developed type of living communities requires the successful emergence of sense-perception to delineate successfully causal efficacy in the external environment; and it also requires its relapse into a reflex suitable to the community. We thus obtain the more flexible communities of low-grade minds, or even living cells, which possess some power of adaptation to the chance details of remote environment.

Finally mankind also uses a more artificial symbolism, obtained chiefly by concentrating on a certain selection of sense-perceptions, such as words for example. In this case, there is a chain of derivations of symbol from symbol whereby finally the local relations, between the final symbol and the ultimate meaning, are entirely lost. Thus these derivative symbols, obtained as it were by arbitrary association, are really the results of reflex action suppressing the intermediate portions of the chain. We may use the word 'association' when there is this suppression of intermediate links.

This derivative symbolism, employed by mankind, is not in general mere indication of meaning, in which every common feature shared by symbol and meaning has been lost. In every effective symbolism there are certain æsthetic features shared in common. The meaning acquires emotion and feeling directly excited by the symbol. This is the whole basis of the art of literature, namely that emotions and feelings directly excited by the words should fitly intensify our emotions and feelings arising from contemplation of the meaning. Further in language there is a certain vagueness of symbolism. A word has a symbolic association with its own history, its other meanings, and with its general status in current literature. Thus a word gathers emotional signification from its emotional history in the past; and this is transferred symbolically to its meaning in present use.

The same principle holds for all the more artificial sorts of human symbolism:—for example, in religious art. Music is particularly adapted for this symbolic transfer of emotions, by reason of the strong emotions which it generates on its own account. These strong emotions at once overpower any sense that its own local relations are of any importance. The only importance of the local arrangement of an orchestra is to enable us to hear the music. We do not listen to the music in order to gain a just appreciation of how the orchestra is situated. When we hear the hoot of a motor car, exactly the converse situation arises. Our only interest in the hoot is to determine a definite locality as the seat of causal efficacy determining the future.

This consideration of the symbolic transference of emotion raises another question. In the case of sense-perception, we may ask whether the æsthetic emotion associated with it is derivative from it or merely concurrent with it. For example, the sound waves by their causal efficacy may produce in the body a state of pleasurable æsthetic emotion, which is then symbolically transferred to the sense-perception of the sounds. In the case of music, having regard to the fact that deaf people do not enjoy music, it seems that the emotion is almost entirely the product of the musical sounds. But the human body is causally affected by the ultra-violet rays of the solar spectrum in ways which do not issue in any sensation of colour. Nevertheless such rays produce a decided emotional effect. Also even sounds, just below or just above the limit of audibility, seem to add an emotional tinge to a volume of audible sound. This whole question of the symbolic transfer of emotion lies at the base of any theory of the æsthetics of art. For example, it gives the reason for the importance of a rigid suppression of irrelevant detail. For emotions inhibit each other, or intensify each other. Harmonious emotion means a complex of emotions mutually intensifying; whereas the irrelevant details supply emotions which, because of their irrelevance, inhibit the main effect. Each little emotion directly arising out of some subordinate detail refuses to accept its status as a detached fact in our consciousness. It insists on its symbolic transfer to the unity of the main effect.

Thus symbolism, including the symbolic transference by which it is effected, is merely one exemplification of the fact that a unity of experience arises out of the confluence of many components. This unity of experience is complex, so as to be capable of analysis. The components of experience are not a structureless collection indiscriminately brought together. Each component by its very nature stands in a certain potential scheme of relationships to the other components. It is the transformation of this potentiality into real unity which constitutes that actual concrete fact which is an act of experience. But in transformation from potentiality to actual fact inhibitions, intensifications, directions of attention toward, directions of attention away from, emotional outcomes, purposes, and other elements of experience may arise. Such elements are also true components of the act of experience; but they are not necessarily determined by the primitive phases of experience from which the final product arises. An act of experience is what a complex organism comes to, in its character of being one thing. Also its various parts, its molecules, and its living cells, as they pass on to new occasions of their existence, take a new colour from the fact that in their immediate past they have been contributory elements to this dominant unity of experience, which in its turn reacts upon them.

Thus mankind by means of its elaborate system of symbolic transference can achieve miracles of sensitiveness to a distant environment, and to a problematic future. But it pays the penalty, by reason of the dangerous fact that each symbolic transference may involve an arbitrary imputation of unsuitable characters. It is not true, that the mere workings of nature in any particular organism are in all respects favorable either to the existence of that organism, or to its happiness, or to the progress of the society in which the organism finds itself. The melancholy experience of men makes this warning a platitude. No elaborate community of elaborate organisms could exist unless its systems of symbolism were in general successful. Codes, rules of behaviour, canons of art, are attempts to impose systematic action which on the whole will promote favourable symbolic interconnections. As a community changes, all such rules and canons require revision in the light of reason. The object to be obtained has two aspects; one is the subordination of the community to the individuals composing it, and the other is the subordination of the individuals to the community. Free men obey the rules which they themselves have made. Such rules will be found in general to impose on society behaviour in reference to a symbolism which is taken to refer to the ultimate purposes for which the society exists.

It is the first step in sociological wisdom, to recognize that the major advances in civilization are processes which all but wreck the societies in which they occur:—like unto an arrow in the hand of a child. The art of free society consists first in the maintenance of the symbolic code; and secondly in fearlessness of revision, to secure that the code serves those purposes which satisfy an enlightened reason. Those societies which cannot combine reverence to their symbols with freedom of revision, must ultimately decay either from anarchy, or from the slow atrophy of a life stifled by useless shadows.